Oceanic Whitetip Sharks and Pilot Fish

by Kari Schuetz

BELLWETHER MEDIA • MINNEAPOLIS, MN

17.95

CP

3/19

Note to Librarians, Teachers, and Parents:

Blastoff! Readers are carefully developed by literacy experts and combine standards-based content with developmentally appropriate text.

Level 1 provides the most support through repetition of high-frequency words, light text, predictable sentence patterns, and strong visual support.

Level 2 offers early readers a bit more challenge through varied simple sentences, increased text load, and less repetition of high-frequency words.

Level 3 advances early-fluent readers toward fluency through increased text and concept load, less reliance on visuals, longer sentences, and more literary language.

Level 4 builds reading stamina by providing more text per page, increased use of punctuation, greater variation in sentence patterns, and increasingly challenging vocabulary.

Level 5 encourages children to move from "learning to read" to "reading to learn" by providing even more text, varied writing styles, and less familiar topics.

Whichever book is right for your reader, Blastoff! Readers are the perfect books to build confidence and encourage a love of reading that will last a lifetime!

This edition first published in 2019 by Bellwether Media, Inc.

No part of this publication may be reproduced in whole or in part without written permission of the publisher. For information regarding permission, write to Bellwether Media, Inc., Attention: Permissions Department, 6012 Blue Circle Drive, Minnetonka, MN 55343.

Library of Congress Cataloging-in-Publication Data

Names: Schuetz, Kari, author.
Title: Oceanic Whitetip Sharks and Pilot Fish / by Kari Schuetz.
Description: Minneapolis, MN : Bellwether Media, Inc., [2019] | Series:
   Blastoff! Readers. Animal Tag Teams | Audience: Ages 5-8. | Audience: K to
   grade 3. | Includes bibliographical references and index.
Identifiers: LCCN 2018033938 (print) | LCCN 2018034869 (ebook) | ISBN
   9781681036878 (ebook) | ISBN 9781626179578 (hardcover : alk. paper)
Subjects: LCSH: Mutualism (Biology)–Juvenile literature. | Oceanic whitetip
   shark–Behavior–Juvenile literature. | Carangidae–Behavior–Juvenile
   literature.
Classification: LCC QL638.G7 (ebook) | LCC QL638.G7 S385 2019 (print) | DDC
   577.8/52–dc23
LC record available at https://lccn.loc.gov/2018033938

Editor: Betsy Rathburn   Designer: Brittany McIntosh

Printed in the United States of America, North Mankato, MN

Table of Contents

Swimming Together

An oceanic whitetip shark follows a **school** of tuna. The **predator** is hungry for a fish dinner.

Pilot fish swim beside the shark. They are the after-dinner cleanup crew!

Oceanic whitetips and pilot fish swim in warm waters around the world. They stay together in the open ocean.

Tag Team Range

= oceanic whitetip shark and pilot fish range

Symbiosis keeps the fish from becoming **prey** for the sharks!

dorsal
fin

pectoral
fin

Oceanic whitetips are big, gray sharks with white on most of their fin tips.

These sharks have large, rounded **dorsal fins** on their backs. Their sides have paddle-shaped **pectoral fins**.

Oceanic Whitetip Shark Profile

type: fish
length: up to 13 feet (4 meters)
weight: up to 370 pounds (168 kilograms)
life span: up to 22 years

Oceanic whitetips hunt small fish and many other ocean animals. They bite at prey.

They also open their mouths and
swim through groups of prey.
During **feeding frenzies**,
these **carnivores** become
deadly attackers!

Fearless Fish

Pilot fish are long, striped fish.
They have bluish bodies with
dark bands.

They have rounded heads and **forked** tails. Their front dorsal fins have short points.

Pilot Fish Profile

type: fish
length: up to 2 feet (0.6 meters)
weight: 1.1 pounds (0.5 kilograms)
life span: up to 3 years

The fish swim close to sharks, rays, and sea turtles.

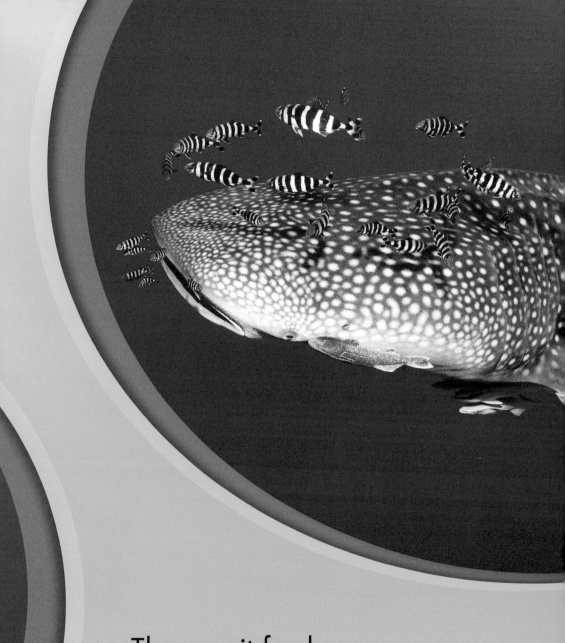

They wait for larger
carnivores to hunt and eat
prey. Then, they finish up
the leftovers!

Helping Each Other

Oceanic whitetips act like **bodyguards** for pilot fish. They scare other ocean predators away.

In return, the fish eat harmful **parasites** that attach themselves to the sharks.

The fish also help the sharks have healthy smiles. They offer regular teeth cleanings.

Without the fish, the sharks have no way to get rid of food stuck between their teeth!

Tag Team Trades

oceanic whitetip sharks

provide meals

give protection

pilot fish

eat pests

clean teeth

When side by side,
oceanic whitetips
and pilot fish support
one another.

The sharks keep the fish alive and fed. The fish keep the sharks in good health. Each animal gives and receives!

Glossary

bodyguards—protectors

carnivores—animals that only eat meat

dorsal fins—fins on the backs of fish

feeding frenzies—events in which predators get excited about prey; during a feeding frenzy, a predator will bite at anything that moves.

forked—having two branches

parasites—living things that use other living things to survive; parasites harm their hosts.

pectoral fins—the front fins on a fish's sides

predator—an animal that hunts other animals for food

prey—animals that are hunted by other animals for food

school—a group of fish

symbiosis—a close relationship between very different living things

To Learn More

AT THE LIBRARY

Hanáčková, Pavla. *Amazing Animal Friendships: Odd Couples in Nature*. Brighton, England: Salariya, 2017.

Rake, Jody S. *Oceanic Whitetip Sharks*. North Mankato, Minn.: Capstone Press, 2019.

Zayarny, Jack. *Symbiosis*. New York, N.Y.: Smartbook Media, Inc., 2017.

ON THE WEB

FACTSURFER

Factsurfer.com gives you a safe, fun way to find more information.

1. Go to www.factsurfer.com.

2. Enter "oceanic whitetip sharks and pilot fish" into the search box.

3. Click the "Surf" button and select your book cover to see a list of related web sites.

Index